notes

William Shakespeare's

Macbeth

Text by
Rebecca McKinlay Sheinberg
(B.A., University of St. Thomas)
Department of English
Contemporary Learning Center High School
Houston, Texas

Illustrations by
Thomas E. Cantillon

 Research & Education Association

MAXnotes™ for
MACBETH

Printed in the United States of America

Library of Congress Catalog Card Number 94-65965

International Standard Book Number 0-87891-944-9

MAXnotes™ is a trademark of
Research & Education Association, Piscataway, New Jersey 08854

What **MAXnotes**™ *Will Do for You*

This book is intended to help you absorb the essential contents and features of William Shakespeare's *Macbeth* and to help you gain a thorough understanding of the work. The book has been designed to do this more quickly and effectively than any other study guide.

For best results, this **MAXnotes** book should be used as a companion to the actual work, not instead of it. The interaction between the two will greatly benefit you.

To help you in your studies, this book presents the most up-to-date interpretations of every section of the actual work, followed by questions and fully explained answers that will enable you to analyze the material critically. The questions also will help you to test your understanding of the work and will prepare you for discussions and exams.

Meaningful illustrations are included to further enhance your understanding and enjoyment of the literary work. The illustrations are designed to place you into the mood and spirit of the work's settings.

The **MAXnotes** also include summaries, character lists, explanations of plot, and chapter-by-chapter analyses. A biography of the author and discussion of the work's historical context will help you put this literary piece into the proper perspective of what is taking place.

The use of this study guide will save you the hours of preparation time that would ordinarily be required to arrive at a complete grasp of this work of literature. You will be well-prepared for classroom discussions, homework, and exams. The guidelines that are included for writing papers and reports on various topics will prepare you for any added work which may be assigned.

The **MAXnotes** will take your grades "to the max."

Dr. Max Fogiel
Program Director

Contents

**Each scene includes List of Characters,
Summary, Analysis, Study Questions and
Answers, and Suggested Essay Topics.**

SECTION ONE

Introduction

The Life and Work of William Shakespeare

William Shakespeare (1564–1616) is generally considered to be the greatest playwright and poet that has ever lived. His appeal is universal and his works have been translated, read, and analyzed throughout the world. Shakespeare wrote 154 sonnets, many poems, and 37 plays which have been grouped into comedies, histories, and tragedies.

Shakespeare's plays combine natural human conflict with dramatic flair producing entertainment that appeals to the audiences of today as well as the audiences for which they were written. Shakespeare understood human nature, and he created characters that portrayed human tragedy and human comedy. Some of his characters were fantastic and unworldly, yet they brought to the stage the truth that mere mortals could not.

Shakespeare was born in Stratford-Upon-Avon, in England. The exact date of his birth is unknown; however, records indicate he was baptized on April 26, 1564, at Holy Trinity Church. Traditionally, a baby was baptized about three days after birth, which would make Shakespeare's birthday April 23, 1564.

His father, John Shakespeare, was from the yeoman class and his mother, Mary Arden, was from a higher class known as the gentry class. The marriage raised John's status in town and the Shakespeare family enjoyed prominence and success in Stratford. This is verified through John Shakespeare's landholding and his status as an alderman.

William was the third child of eight, and it can be assumed he attended the local grammar school in Stratford. School ran for nine hours a day, year-round, and strict discipline was enforced. Shakespeare probably attended school until he was 15, which was customary for the time.

Around this time, Shakespeare's father was experiencing financial difficulty, and William probably took a job to help the family. His father was a glover and dealer in commodities, and Shakespeare may have assisted his father in his business, but it is presumed Shakespeare worked in a variety of jobs.

At 18, Shakespeare had an affair with Anne Hathaway, who was eight years his senior. They married, and six months later they had a child. Susanna Shakespeare was born in May of 1583 and in 1585 twins, Hamnet and Judith, were born to the Shakespeares. Little is known of that period except that the twins were christened in February 1585.

Shakespeare's life became public record in 1592 through a pamphlet written by Robert Greene with criticism of Shakespeare's work as an actor as well as a playwright. After Greene's death, the letter appeared again. Almost as quickly as it appeared, Greene's publisher printed an apology to Shakespeare.

From 1592 to 1594 many public theaters were closed due to the plague, and Shakespeare wrote poems and sonnets during this period. In 1594, he became a shareholder in a company of actors known as the Lord Chamberlain's Men. From 1594 to 1608 he was completely involved in the theatre.

His time in the years 1608 to 1616 was divided between the theater and his family. Shakespeare's success as a playwright and shareholder afforded him the luxury of owning homes in London and Stratford. His son Hamnet died at the age of 11. Judith had three boys, but all died. His daughter Susanna had one child, Elizabeth, who had no children. The recorded date for Shakespeare's death is April 23, 1616. He is buried inside the Stratford parish church. Shakespeare's last direct descendant, his granddaughter, Elizabeth, died in 1670.

Historical Background

Shakespeare drew from many sources when he wrote—the *Holingshed Chronicles of England* was one of these. From this source he drew much of his historical knowledge, as Holingshed was the definitive historical source of that time. The story of Macbeth comes from this source. However, Shakespeare changed several characters to meet the theatrical purpose of the play. In Holingshed's account Macbeth is older than Duncan, but Shakespeare reverses their ages and Duncan is portrayed as the older of the two.

Macbeth was written especially for James I and was performed in 1606. James I was King of Scotland when he came to the English throne; his descendants can be traced back to Banquo. In Shakespeare's Macbeth, often referred to in theater circles as "The Scottish Play," Banquo is portrayed as an honorable man who promotes goodness and fairness. In this way, Shakespeare was keenly aware of his audience and his political responsibilities. His plays reflect not only timeless conflicts and resolutions, but a view of the Elizabethan society.

The society in which Shakespeare lived was reflected in the characters he wrote about. London was a crowded city teaming with aristocrats, working class people, and indigents—it was a hub of activity. By today's standards the sanitation was very poor, and there were frequent epidemics of the plague. The city was infested with rats, and the fleas on the rats caused the Bubonic plague. There were no sewers, only open drains in the middle of the street. The conditions were difficult; however, the spirit of the people prevailed. It was in this society that Shakespeare wrote and created his characters.

Shakespearean Theatre

The support of theatre in England varied depending on who was the reigning monarch. Queen Elizabeth I (1533 - 1603) was the monarch when Shakespeare came into the public eye. Elizabeth supported the theater and the company performed at the castle on a regular basis. She reigned until her death in 1603 when James I became ruler.

James I was also an avid supporter of the theatre. Shakespeare's company, "Lord Chamberlain's Men," came under royal patronage and were subsequently known as "the King's Men." However, the local London government felt that actors and theater were improper. Therefore, no theaters were allowed to be built within the city limits. These restrictions did not keep the London people from the theaters, however, and by 1600 there were more theaters than ever built on the outskirts of London.

The Globe theater was built by Cuthbert Burbage in 1599 for the Lord Chamberlain's Men. When Burbage could not obtain a lease for the original theater, it was moved to a new site in Southwark, on the south side of the Thames River. The construction of the Globe was a joint venture between the Burbage brothers and the actors of the Lord Chamberlain's Men.

The Globe was a three-story structure with at least five sides and no roof over the stage. The roof extended around the gallery that encircled the theatre. Each floor had seats that encircled a stage that was built in the center. Behind the stage were dressing rooms and space to store scenery and props. There were no curtains used to conceal the stage, only a curtain to separate the backstage area from the stage. Very few props were used. In the front center portion of the stage was a trap door used to enable a person to vanish (or to allow a ghost to appear.)

A flag was flown from the front portion of the roof to announce when a play was to be presented. When patrons saw the flag, they knew there would be a performance that day; there were no performances at night, as there was no artificial lighting at the Globe. The theater was small—approximately 30 feet in height, 86 feet in diameter, 56 feet for the open courtyard, and about 40 feet for the stage itself. The patrons either stood in the courtyard and watched the play, or paid more and sat in the gallery.

The actors were flexible and dedicated to the craft of acting. They actors had a major responsibility to convey the purpose of the drama to the audience. The actors supported the written word through their portrayal of the characters. The dialogue and the language supported the setting of the scene within the play, as scenery was very limited. Shakespeare's language provided the scenery for the play. When the scene was changed to an evening scene, the actor would carry a torch in to indicate that it was night. The audience of the time was accustomed to this type of staging.

The theater was a much more intimate setting than the theaters of today. The patrons would voice their opinions during a production of a play; some even threw vegetables at the actors on the stage. The theater gained a reputation for rowdy behavior and aristocratic society did not consider theater a respectable part of Elizabethan society.

The Globe burned down in a fire in 1613, when a cannon was fired during a performance and the thatched roof over the gallery caught on fire. It was rebuilt that year, but in 1644 the structure was torn down when theatres were closed due to the government ban on theatres.

Master List of Characters

Three Witches—*Evil prophets that guide Macbeth's destiny with incomplete information regarding his future*

Macbeth—*Thane of Glamis, later King of Scotland*

Lady Macbeth—*Macbeth's wife and supporter of her husband's quest for power*

Duncan—*King of Scotland*

Malcolm—*Duncan's older son*

Donalbain—*Duncan's younger son*

Banquo—*General in the Scottish Army and Macbeth's friend*

Fleance—*Banquo's son who is seen as a threat by Macbeth*

Macduff—*Nobleman of Scotland and rival of Macbeth*

Lady Macduff—*Macduff's wife*

Son—*Macduff's son*

Lennox and Ross—*Noblemen of Scotland that support Malcolm's fight against Macbeth*

Angus—*Nobleman of Scotland and supporter against Macbeth*

Menteith and Caithness—*Noblemen of Scotland in Malcolm's English Army*

Porter—*servant at Macbeth's castle*

Murderers—*Macbeth's hired killers*

Hecate—*Goddess of the Witches*

Apparitions—*Visions conjured up by the Witches to inform Macbeth of what he should fear for the future*

Doctor and Gentlewoman—*Servants that witness Lady Macbeth's sleepwalking*

Seyton—*An Officer in Macbeth's Army*

Siward—*General in the English army fighting with Malcolm*

Young Siward—*Siward's son in the English army with Malcolm*

Captain—*Soldier in Duncan's military that reports on Macbeth's success in the battle against Macdonwald*

Summary of the Play

The play begins on an open stretch of land in medieval Scotland. Three Witches enter and give the prophecy that the civil war will end that day and that at sunset they will meet Macbeth. The Witches are summoned to leave, but they do not leave without stating that what is normally "fair" will be "foul," and what is "foul" will be "fair."

King Duncan learns that Macbeth has been victorious and has defeated Macdonwald. The Thane of Cawdor has betrayed Duncan and is accused of being a traitor. Duncan orders the Thane of Cawdor's execution and announces that Macbeth will receive the title of Thane of Cawdor.

Macbeth and Banquo leave the battlefield and meet the Witches. The Witches state the prophecy that Macbeth will be Thane of Cawdor and king and that Banquo will be the father of kings, but not king himself. Macbeth has been victorious on the battlefield and the war is at an end—to what greatness should he now aspire?

The Witches spark the ambitious nature in Macbeth, as he knows his rise to power would greatly be enhanced by being named Thane of Cawdor. After the Witches vanish, Ross and Angus arrive and announce that Macbeth has been named Thane of Cawdor. Banquo is skeptical of the Witches, but Macbeth, driven by a desire for power, considers killing Duncan to gain the crown. Macbeth is overwhelmed by the image, yet his desire for power is still present, as stated in a letter he sends to Lady Macbeth.

Lady Macbeth encourages Macbeth to act on his thoughts, telling him that she will guide and support his plan to kill King Duncan. While Duncan is visiting Inverness, Macbeth's castle, Macbeth kills Duncan as he sleeps. After the murder is discovered, Macbeth kills the servants, whom he accuses of Duncan's murder. Duncan's sons, fearing for their own lives, flee Scotland. Macbeth is crowned king.

Banquo raises suspicions that Macbeth killed Duncan.

Macbeth hires two men to kill Banquo and his son Fleance, whom Macbeth fears will become king, as the Witches foretold. Banquo is killed, but Fleance escapes.

The Witches conjure a spell, and Apparitions reveal to Macbeth three prophecies that will affect his future. He is told to beware of Macduff, that no man born of woman can harm him, and he will not be conquered until the forest at Birnam marches to Dunsinane. Macbeth is also shown a procession of kings with the last king looking in a mirror—the reflection is that of Banquo.

Macbeth orders Macduff's family to be murdered and leaves for England to confront Macduff. When Macduff hears of the massacre of his family he vows to seek revenge on Macbeth. He joins Malcolm in his quest to depose Macbeth.

The army proceeds in camouflage by carrying a branch from Birnam Wood into battle. Alarmed by this, Macbeth fears the Witches' prophecy will come true. Macbeth is told of Lady Macbeth's death by her own hands and he laments the nature of his life.

Macbeth fights Macduff, and Macbeth boasts that he cannot be killed by any man born of woman. Macduff informs Macbeth that he was surgically removed from his mother's womb and thus was not born of woman. Macduff kills Macbeth in battle and hails Malcolm as King of Scotland. Malcolm vows to restore Scotland to a peaceful country.

Estimated Reading Time

The time needed to read *Macbeth* depends on the familiarity of the reader with the language of the Elizabethan Era. The notes and glossary of the text being used should serve as a guide to the reader. A recorded version of the play would serve as a source for pronunciation and aid the reader with inflection and intent of the words.

Since Shakespeare wrote in blank verse, a form of un-rhymed poetry, there is a rhythm to the reading that becomes easier to follow as the reader moves through the play. The estimated reading time is approximately 12 to 14 hours.

Act I

New Characters:

Three Witches: *evil prophets; also known as the Weird Sisters*

Duncan: *King of Scotland*

Malcolm: *Duncan's son*

Captain: *a wounded Scottish-soldier*

Lennox: *nobleman of Scotland*

Ross: *nobleman of Scotland*

Macbeth: *Duncan's cousin and General in the military*

Banquo: *soldier and Macbeth's friend*

Angus: *nobleman of Scotland*

Lady Macbeth: *Macbeth's wife*

Summary

Scene 1

The play opens on a bleak and lonely stretch of land in Scotland. Three Witches report that the battle Macbeth is fighting will be over by sunset; they plan to meet with

Macbeth on the barren battlefield, or "heath," at that time.
The setting is enhanced by an approaching thunder storm
and three Witches foretelling of the evil they foresee for
the future: "Fair is foul, and foul is fair," what is good will
be bad and what is bad will be good.

Scene 2

The king of Scotland, Duncan, learns of the events of

the battle from the wounded Captain that has just returned from the battlefield. The Captain informs Duncan
that Macbeth has defeated Macdonwald, the Norwegian
army, and the Thane of Cawdor. Macbeth is reported to
be brave and fearless. The Captain states the conflict was
resolved by Macbeth. The King orders the immediate execution of the traitorous Thane of Cawdor and names
Macbeth as the new Thane of Cawdor. Duncan sends Ross
to announce this to Macbeth on the battlefield.

Scene 3

The Witches are on the battlefield discussing the evil
and disruptive deeds they have been doing. The First
Witch had a disagreement with a sailor's wife because the
wife would not give her any of the chestnuts she was eat-
ing. This angers the Witches and they decide to torture
the woman's husband by creating a windstorm that will
blow his ship to all points on the compass. The storm will
be so intense he will not be able to rest. The first Witch
says, "I'll drain him dry as hay." She then brags about the
"pilot's thumb," or small bone, she has as a charm. The
Witches hear a drum and the approach of Macbeth.

Macbeth and Banquo enter and are unaware of the
Witches at first. Macbeth's first line in the play, "So foul
and fair a day I have not seen," alludes to the initial prophecy of the Three Witches. Banquo then spies the Witches,
but he is unable to determine if they are men or women:
"You should be women, and yet your beards forbid me to
interpret that you are so." The Witches then greet Macbeth
with his current title, Thane of Glamis, and two titles he is
yet to have, Thane of Cawdor and King. Macbeth is perplexed by their greeting because he knows that both the
Thane of Cawdor and King are still alive.

Banquo, hearing such a good fortune for this friend, inquires as to his own fate. He is told that he will be lesser and greater than Macbeth; even though he will never be king, his sons will. The Witches then dissolve into the air, leaving Banquo to wonder if they were real or just an hallucination.

Ross and Angus greet them with the news that Macbeth has been named Thane of Cawdor by Duncan.

Banquo and Macbeth are surprised and contemplate the evil nature of the Witches. Macbeth is eager for power; however, Banquo warns him of the evil nature of the Witches and that the outcome of his actions could be disastrous to him.

Scene 4

Duncan inquires if the Thane of Cawdor has been executed and expresses regret as to giving the order to have him killed. Macbeth enters and they exchange accolades. Duncan names his own son, Malcolm to succeed him as king. This creates a conflict for Macbeth as Malcolm is another obstacle to overcome toward his goal to succeed Duncan as king.

> The Prince of Cumberland! That is a step
> On which I must fall down or else o'erleap
> For in my way it lies. Stars, hide your fires;
> Let no light see my black and deep desires.

Duncan plans to visit Inverness, Macbeth's castle, and the scene ends with Macbeth leaving to prepare for Duncan's visit.

Scene 5

Lady Macbeth has received a letter from Macbeth stating that he has been named Thane of Cawdor. The letter reveals his ambition to be king and the prophecy given by the Witches. Lady Macbeth discloses her ambitious nature and vows to help Macbeth succeed in his ambition to be crowned King. She receives word that King Duncan will be arriving soon and is perplexed because Macbeth has not informed her himself. Macbeth arrives

and they concur that by any means he should be crowned
King:

>Come, you spririts
>Thast tend on mortal thoughts, unsex me here
>And fill me from the crown to the toe top-full
>Of direst cruelty! Make thick my blood...

Lady Macbeth tells him he should be a gracious host and
they will speak on the matter later that evening.

Scene 6

Duncan arrives with his entourage and Lady Macbeth welcomes him upon his arrival. Duncan is eager to meet with Macbeth as he and Lady Macbeth exchange greetings.

Scene 7

Macbeth gives a dinner for Duncan and his guests that evening. During the dinner, Macbeth leaves and begins

to contemplate the plan he and Lady Macbeth have dis-
cussed. He struggles with his conscience and the fear of
eternal damnation if he murders Duncan. This internal
conflict is reinforced because Macbeth is Duncan's cousin,
he is a beloved king, and Duncan is a guest in his home:

> First, as I am his kinsman and his subject,
> Strong both against the deed; then as his host,
> Who should against his murderer shut the door,
> Not bear the knife myself.

Lady Macbeth calls Macbeth a coward and implies that
he is less than a man for faltering in his plan to murder
Duncan. Her resolute desire and quest for power sway
Macbeth to agree with her and he decides to go through
with the plan.

Analysis

Introducing the play with the Witches in the first scene
creates an evil tone and mysterious setting; something sinister is about to happen. Witches were traditionally
thought of in Elizabethan times as evil and connected to
devil's work. The supernatural was feared and respected.
The Witches statement, "Fair is foul, and foul is fair",
clearly depicts that the events in the play will be evil and
destructive. The thunderstorm and filthy air reinforce the
evil prediction of the Witches and clearly indicates to the
audience that a conflict between man and nature/good
and evil exists within the world of the play. Scene 1 creates the atmosphere of evil that will continue throughout
the play.

Duncan is portrayed as a concerned and interested
ruler. The Captain reports the events in the battle and he
characterizes Macbeth as a worthy and loyal subject to

Duncan. The King is filled with gratitude and respect for Macbeth and the Captain. Duncan's compassion, however, is limited to his loyal subjects, as he orders the Thane of Cawdor's execution immediately upon hearing of him being a traitor.

Macbeth's actions in battle, by contrast, are barbaric and aggressive. He not only killed the enemy, but he cut him from his navel to his mouth, and cut off the victims head and placed it on the "battlements." This scene reveals the historical data needed for the introduction of the conflicts Macbeth creates and faces in his struggle for power. At this point Macbeth is viewed as a noble, loyal subject fighting battles victoriously for the King and Scotland. However, his actions on the battlefield reveal him to be a ruthless killer.

The Witches begin Scene 3 exhibiting the powers they possess; however, they are limited in these powers. They can create situations that will cause destruction (such as the storm), but they lack the power to actually sink the sailor's ship. The audience can infer that Macbeth will create his own havoc because of the prophecy made by the Witches comes true. The Witches guide Macbeth's fate through their statements. Macbeth states, "So foul and fair a day I have not seen," echoing the Witches' lines in the first scene of the play. This repetition links Macbeth to the Witches. The audience makes a logical connection that Macbeth will be linked to the evil conflict in the world of the play.

Macbeth and Banquo meet the Witches on the field, and the Witches greet Macbeth with three titles. As noted through Banquo's dialogue, Macbeth is clearly startled. Banquo is equally interested in what the future will hold for him. He learns that his sons will be kings, but for him—nothing.

When Duncan's men give Macbeth the news that he is to be the new Thane of Cawdor, Macbeth considers what the Witches have said and becomes concerned about their evil nature. He states his desire to be King, but he ponders over the cost. Banquo questions the evil nature of the Witches' and warns Macbeth to look closer at the Witches predictions before he acts on them.

Duncan feels he may have acted in haste in ordering the death of the first Thane of Cawdor. This demonstrates the king's compassionate character and conscience. Macbeth greets his cousin Duncan with respect and friendship knowing full well he is plotting to take control. When Duncan announces that his son Malcolm will succeed him as king, Macbeth outwardly supports Duncan's decision. However, he is disappointed and knows he must eliminate Duncan and his son Malcolm to become king. Macbeth now struggles with this conflict and ponders what fate may bring.

Out of love for her husband, Lady Macbeth hardens her heart in order to aid him in mudering Duncan. Unlike Macbeth, she pushes aside her conscience when she makes her decision: "Nor heaven peep through the blanket of dark / To cry "Hold, hold!" She also uses the love they share to lend courage when Macbeth falters. Macbeth's success, and therefore her own fate, lies in Macbeth carrying out his homicidal plot.

When Duncan arrives at Inverness his gentle and loving nature is reinforced. He is again seen as a caring King interested in his subjects. This creates empathy for the innocent Duncan, and the image of Macbeth as a loyal trustworthy friend to Duncan begins to change. Macbeth reveals that he has a conscience as he questions his motives for killing Duncan. However, Lady Macbeth questions his manhood, calls him a coward, and coaxes Macbeth to follow through with the plan. She knows Macbeth's weak points and uses them to bolster his convinction. Her desire for Macbeth to be king overcomes her basic human compassion and greed seduces her morality. Macbeth becomes victim to his selfish desire for power.

Study Questions

1. What atmosphere is established in Scene 1?

2. How does Banquo describe the Witches when he first sees them upon the heath?

3. Macbeth is reported to be a valiant soldier in Act I. The line, "Till he unseamed him from the nave to th'chops And fixed his head upon our battlements", paints a different Macbeth. What can you infer from that line?

4. In Scene 1 the Witches say, "Foul is fair and fair is foul." Which characters do you consider fair or foul?

5. Why do you think Shakespeare opened Scene 3 with the Witches discussing an evil deed they have committed?

6. What prophesies do the Witches make for Macbeth and Banquo?

7. What does Lady Macbeth mean when she says of Macbeth, "Yet do I fear thy nature. It is too full o' the milk of human kindness To catch the nearest way"?

8. Macbeth is having second thoughts about killing

Duncan. What are the reasons he gives? Based on these reasons what does he decide?

9. What does Lady Macbeth mean when she says, "Was hope drunk Wherein you dressed yourself? Hath it slept since? And wakes it now to look so green and pale"?

10. What decision does Macbeth make at the end of Act I? What has Lady Macbeth said to influence his decision?

Answers

1. The scene is filled with Witches, thunder and lightning, which creates a dark and sinister atmosphere.

2. He calls them "withered" and "wild" in their attire; "That they look not like the inhabitants o' the' earth;" and that they "should be women...yet [their] beards forbid [him] to interpret that [they] are so."

3. Macbeth is a cold-blooded killer on the battlefield.

4. The Witches are foul because they are evil. Macbeth and Banquo seem to be fair because of their loyalty and bravery. However, Macbeth reveals his plan to murder Duncan and his character is viewed differently. Lady Macbeth is foul. Macdonwald is foul because he is a traitor. The Captain and Duncan are fair because the Captain fought bravely and the King supports him and is compassionate regarding the Captain's injury.

5. The Witches are capable of creating situations that are evil and destructive. However, their powers are limited as they cannot destroy, but they have the

power to create an atmosphere where destruction can easily occur.

6. The Witches state that Macbeth will be Thane of Cawdor and King. They go on to tell Banquo that his son's will be kings.

7. Lady Macbeth feels that Macbeth is kind and he may not be able to overcome his fears to kill Duncan. She fears his conscience will override his ambition to be King.

8. Macbeth is torn between his ambition and his conscience. He gives several reasons why he should not kill Duncan: 1) Duncan is his cousin; 2) He is a loyal subject to the King; 3) Duncan is his friend; 4) Duncan has never abused his royal power; and 5) Duncan is a guest in his home. Based on these reasons, Macbeth decides not to follow through with the murder of Duncan.

9. Lady Macbeth is questioning Macbeth why he has changed his mind about killing Duncan. She is asking him what has happened to his ambition.

10. Lady Macbeth persuades Macbeth to follow through with the plan to murder Duncan. She calls him a coward and less than a man, prodding Macbeth to follow her plan. Macbeth agrees to murder Duncan that night.

Suggested Essay Topics

1. Macbeth struggles with his conscience and the fear of eternal damnation if he murders Duncan. Lady Macbeth's conflict arises when Macbeth's courage begins to falter. Lady Macbeth has great control over

Macbeth's actions. What tactics does she use to gain control over him? Cite examples from Act I. Does she solve her conflict through her actions? Cite examples from Act I.

2. Shakespeare begins *Macbeth* with Witches talking on a barren stretch of land in a thunder storm. This creates a certain atmosphere and mood. What images contributed to the evil atmosphere? Do you feel this mood continues through Act I? Did the actions and dialog of the main characters reinforce this atmosphere?

Act II

New Characters:

Fleance: *Banquo's son*

Porter: *doorman for Macbeth*

Macduff: *nobleman of Scotland*

Donalbain: *Duncan's younger son*

Summary

Scene 1

There is something in the air that disturbs Banquo and Fleance and they cannot sleep. As they discuss the reasons for their inability to sleep, Macbeth joins them. Banquo confesses that he has been dreaming about the prophecy the Witches told them and he is concerned about the evil nature of the Witches. Macbeth responds by saying, "I think not of them." Both agree to discuss the matter at a later date. Banquo and Fleance retire to their chambers to sleep.

As Macbeth, alone in the hall, contemplates the murder he is about to commit, a bloody dagger appears before him:

Is this a dagger which I see before me,
The handle toward my hand? Come let me clutch
thee.
I have thee not, and yet I see thee still...
And on thy blade and dudgeon gouts of blood.

Macbeth is still hesitant about killing Duncan. Once
he hear Lady Macbeth's signal, though, the ringing of the
bell, he no longer delays and proceeds to Duncan's room.

Scene 2

Lady Macbeth is filled with anticipation for Macbeth's safe return and the completion of Duncan's murder. Her fears surface when she is startled by a noise that turns out to be nothing more than an owl screeching. She is concerned that the plot may not be completed and that Macbeth will be discovered before Duncan is murdered.

Lady Macbeth reveals in a soliloquy that when she placed the daggers in Duncan's chamber she considered

killing Duncan herself. However, Duncan looked too much like her father and she could not commit the act herself: "Had he not resembled / My father as he slept, I had done't."

When Macbeth returns he is distraught and regrets the murder he has committed. Macbeth reports to Lady Macbeth that as he murdered Duncan's guards, he heard a voice cry, "Sleep no more! Macbeth hath murdered sleep." In his tormented state, Macbeth leaves the murder scene carrying the bloody daggers.

Lady Macbeth urges him to return the daggers and place them by the slain Duncan, but Macbeth refuses to return to the chamber. Lady Macbeth returns the daggers and stains her hands with Duncan's blood. They hear a knock and retire to their sleeping quarters before the Porter arrives at the door.

Scene 3

Macduff and Lennox have arrived at Macbeth's castle at Inverness at daybreak. The Porter jokes and carries on with Macduff about his drinking and lack of success with women the night before as Macbeth joins them. Macduff leaves Lennox and Macbeth to discuss the violent storm they had the night before.

Macduff rushes back to the courtyard with the news that the king had been murdered. Macbeth and Lennox rush to the chamber and Macduff sounds the alarm. Macbeth confesses when he saw the slain Duncan he was filled with rage and murdered Duncan's guards. He felt they were the murderers because they were smeared with blood and had the daggers in their hands. Confusion and shock ensues and Lady Macbeth faints. Donalbain and Malcolm fear foul play has been committed by someone

close to them: "Where we are, / There's daggers in men's smiles; the nea'er in blood, / The nearer bloody."

Donalbain says he will go to Ireland, while Malcolm agrees to go to England. They flee the castle in fear of their own lives while Macduff, Macbeth, and the others agree to meet to discuss the catastrophe.

Scene 4

The following day Ross and an old man discuss the strange events that have taken place. Ross says that

Duncan's horses became enraged, broke out of their stalls, and ate each other. Other unnatural events are going on with the birds and the weather. They fear all of this has to do with Duncan's murder.

Macduff joins the discussion and it is revealed that Duncan's body has been taken to the family plot at Colmekill and Macbeth has been named to succeed Duncan as King. The coronation will take place at Scone. Ross plans to go to Scone and Macduff leaves for Fife, of which he is Thane. Macduff fears the worst is yet to come.

Analysis

The second act opens with Banquo and his son, Fleance, walking the halls at Inverness, unable to sleep. Banquo has been plagued by dreams of the Witches. As he walks with Fleance, he hands him the sword and dagger he is wearing. Shakespeare uses this scene to fore-shadow Fleance's eventual assumption of his father's role. Symbolically, the torch is being passed from father to son.

Macbeth enters and is confronted by Banquo, who was unable to distinguish him in the dim light. Macbeth greets Banquo as "a friend." This is ironic because in the next act, Macbeth proves to be much less than a friend. They discuss the prophecies of the Witches, Banquo say-ing he has dreamed of them, while Macbeth says he has not thought at all about them. Yet, they are all Macbeth has thought about. Macbeth has planned the murder of the King because of the prophecies.

After Banquo and his son have departed, Macbeth sends his servant to tell his wife to strike the bell when his drink is ready. This is his signal to enter Ducan's chamber and kill him. As he waits, a vision of a dagger appears floating before him. He reaches for it, but is unable to grasp it. He thinks the dagger is a product of his "heat-oppressed brain." The dagger beckons Macbeth toward Duncan's room and it becomes covered in blood as Macbeth approaches the chamber of the sleeping King. Macbeth's conscience creates the vision of the dagger, either to halt his plans by revealing the horror of the act or, as Macbeth believes, to beckon him forward. But, if Macbeth's will were about to falter, Lady Macbeth's signal, the ringing of the bell, provides him with the courage to finish what he has started.

Lady Macbeth greatly anticipates the return of Macbeth from the murderous act. While she waits, she gathers strength from the knowledge that she has drugged the drinks of Duncan's servants. "That which hath made them drunk hath made me bold;/ What hath quenched them hath given me fire!" Because the servants will be unable to stop Macbeth, Lady Macbeth knows that their plot to eliminate the king will be unimpeded. Yet, the act of murder and a guilty conscience cause her to jump at the screeching of an owl. She then refers to the "fatal bellman," a man that rang a bell outside a condemned man's cell encouraging him to confess his sins. She is inferring that Duncan is a condemned man and should repent his sins. Also, she could be referring to Macbeth, as he will be a condemned man if he is caught committing the murder. Even if he is not caught, the murder of Duncan is a sin that condemns Macbeth's soul.

Lady Macbeth asked to be "unsexed" in an earlier scene so that she may have the necessary strength to support Macbeth in his quest for the throne. However, when she placed the daggers by the sleeping Duncan, she was unable to kill him because he looked too much like her father. Her conscience surfaced and she deferred to Macbeth to complete the evil plan.

Having killed Duncan, Macbeth returns to his wife's side in a dazed and confused state. He then tells his wife that as he approached Duncan, one of the servants cried out "Murder" in his sleep. This woke both the servants up. One then said "God bless us!" and the other "Amen!" He is concerned that he could not say "amen" in return. He wanted to, but he found the words stuck in his throat. Macbeth is unable to receive the blessing he desires because of the sin he is about to commit.

After he has killed Duncan, his conscience begins to project voices that he thinks the entire castle can hear. "Still it cried 'Sleep no more!' to all the house;/ 'Glamis hath murdered sleep, and therefore Cawdor/ Shall sleep no more; Macbeth shall sleep no more.'" Macbeth feels so guilty for the act that his mind projects voices that condemn him. He will no longer have the piece of mind that he had before the murder.

Lady Macbeth counsels her husband to ignore the voices that he thinks he has heard because dwelling upon them and the act he has just committed could drive him mad. She also tells him to return the bloody daggers to Duncan's room. Macbeth is unable to face his crime again. so Lady Macbeth takes the daggers back. She returns with her hands now covered with blood like her husband. By having Lady Macbeth handle the daggers and get blood on her hands, Shakespeare is showing that even though she never commits an act of murder, her participation in planning makes her just as guilty.

When they hear the knock at the door, both adjourn to their sleeping quarters to establish an alibi if someone should come looking for them. Macbeth again expresses his regret at killing Duncan when he says, "Wake Duncan with thy knocking! I would thou/ couldst!"

In order to give the audience a moment to recuperate from the heavy drama of the last scene, scene 3 opens with the comic banter of the porter at the door. He talks with Macduff about the effects of drinking on the body. But besides a bit of comedy, the scene also serves to establish a diabolical atmosphere around Macbeth's castle. The porter curses in the "name of Beelzebub." He does not call to God, instead he calls forth the name of the devil. He then hypothesizes as to who is knocking at the door. He names three people who would knock at the gates of Hell; a farmer that hanged himself, an equivocator that commits treason, and a tailor who steals cloth. He even talks about the people who walk the way to the "everlasting bonfire."

These references to Hell serve to show the audience that Macbeth is creating a Hell within Scotland.

Macbeth then enters and Macduff goes to wake the king. While he is gone, Lennox–who arrived with Macduff–tells Macbeth of the turbulent night. The woeful weather outside mimics the horrible events inside Macbeth's castle. Macduff then returns with the news of the king's murder. Macbeth, faking astonishment, rushes off with Lennox to see the body. He later claims to have slain the servants, whom he had implicated in the murder, in a fit of rage over their heinous deed. Lady Macbeth continues her charade by fainting at the news.

Duncan's sons, Malcolm and Donalbain, fear that the real killers were not the servants, but someone closer to them. They fear that whoever is ambitious enough to kill the king will come after them as well. "This murderous shaft that's shot/Hath not yet lighted, and our safest way/ Is to avoid the aim." Malcolm flees to England and Donalbain to Ireland. Once they have fled Scotland, they are considered guilty in their own father's murder.

There is a time lapse between the last two scenes of the second act. The Old Man and Ross discuss the events that have transpired over the last few days. They talk of strange portents and how ambition is the ruin of men. The audience can infer that Macbeth's ambition will ruin him. This last scene also shows how Macbeth is still unable to look upon the body of Duncan. He goes to Scone to be crowned instead of Colmekill for the funeral.

Study Questions

1. What are Banquo's concerns about the Witches prophecy? What is Macbeth's response?

2. What does Macbeth see when Banquo and Fleance leave and what does he say about it?

3. What was Lady Macbeth unable to do in Duncan's chamber? Why?

4. What was Macbeth's reaction when he returned from Duncan's chamber? What did he say?

5. Who was sleeping in the second chamber? Why did Shakespeare include that information in the play?

6. Macbeth is unable to return to Duncan's chamber with the bloody daggers. Why do you think he fears going back?

7. What does Lennox say to Macbeth about the previous night?

8. Who discovers that Duncan has been murdered?

9. Why does Macbeth say he has murdered the guards?

10. Why do Donalbain and Malcolm leave? Where do they say they are going?

Answers

1. He has had bad dreams about the Witches and part of what they said has come true. Macbeth says he has not thought about them. Banquo would like to discuss the matter with Macbeth.

2. He sees a bloody dagger floating before him. He says that it is only a dream.

3. She was unable to kill Duncan because he looked like her father.

4. He was upset and feeling guilt. He said that "it was a sorry sight." He also stated that he had murdered sleep and he could not say amen when he needed to.

5. Donalbain was sleeping. This puts suspicion on him.

6. He cannot face the murder that he has committed. He feels too much guilt.

7. Lennox said that there was a bad storm and he has never seen one this fierce in his life.

8. Macduff discovers Duncan's slain body.

9. Macbeth says he murdered the guards because felt they killed Duncan. He was so angry and grief stricken he could not control his rage.

10. Donalbain and Malcolm because they fear for their own lives. Donalbain goes to Ireland and Malcolm goes to England.

Suggested Essay Topics

1. The Witches are characters that have a powerful impact on the play, but have very few lines. Banquo says that he cannot sleep because he is thinking about them. Macbeth says that he has not thought about them at all. How do the characters of Macbeth and Banquo differ and what influence have the Witches had on each character?

2. Macbeth is alone while Lady Macbeth returns the bloody daggers when he says, "Will all great Neptune's ocean wash this blood clean from my hand? No, this my hand will rather The multitudinous seas incarnadine, Making the green one red." Lady Macbeth returns will blood on her hands as well. What does the blood symbolize? Cite examples from the play.

Act III

New Characters:

Murderers: *hired killers*

Hecate: *a Witch*

Summary

Scene 1

Banquo says that the prophecy has come true for Macbeth. He would like the prophecy the Witches made about his sons to come true also. Banquo feels that he must appear loyal to Macbeth, yet he does not trust him.

Macbeth questions Banquo as to his schedule for the day and says to Banquo to be sure and join them at the banquet that evening. Banquo and his son plan to go out riding for the day. Macbeth is worried that the prophecy of Banquo's sons being kings will come true. His reign will be barren if his sons do not succeed him. Macbeth hires two men to murder Banquo and Fleance.

Scene 2

Lady Macbeth questions Macbeth as to his plans, but he does not inform her of the plan to kill Banquo and

Fleance. She encourages Macbeth not to think about Banquo or the events that have taken place. Macbeth tells her not to worry.

Scene 3

A third murderer joins the two Macbeth had hired in the previous scene. They wait along the path that Banquo and his son travel. As they approach, walking their horses,

the murderers jump out. Banquo is killed, but Fleance is able to escape.

Scene 4

At the banquet, Macbeth learns that the murderers have not been entirely successful. They killed Banquo, but Fleance was able to escape. Macbeth takes joy in learning that Banquo is dead, because he cannot produce any more sons. He says he will deal with the matter of Fleance later.

As Macbeth is seated at the banquet table, the ghost of Banquo appears. This startles Macbeth and he responds to the vision. No one but Macbeth can see the ghost. Lady Macbeth assures her guests that Macbeth has had these attacks since he was a child and it will soon pass. She urges Macbeth to resume his role as host. As quickly as he offers his apology to his guest, the ghost appears again. Macbeth loses control and Lady Macbeth fears he will confess to the murder of Duncan. She asks her guest to leave quickly. The ghost disappears and Macbeth ques-

tions why Macduff did not attend the banquet. Macbeth feels he must consult with the Witches again to gain information about the future.

Scene 5

Hecate is another Witch that Shakespeare introduces to the audience. Hecate is upset because the other Witches did not consul her before they spoke to Macbeth. Hecate assures them she will conjure a spell that will lead

Macbeth to a disastrous fate. She sends them to cast the spell and prepare the charm, as Macbeth plans to visit them soon.

Scene 6

Lennox says to a Lord that he feels it is a pity that Banquo was killed. He goes on to imply that Macbeth is responsible for both Duncan's and Banquo's deaths; even though the general consensus is that Fleance killed his own father, as did Malcolm and Donalbain. Lennox does not believe either had anything to do with the deaths of their fathers. Macbeth has stolen Malcolm's birthright to be king and Malcolm is in England trying to secure an army to gain his birthright back. Macduff has gone to join in his effort. Lennox and the Lord hope that Malcolm will be successful in restoring peace to Scotland.

Analysis

Banquo says Macbeth has attained all the Witches said he would and at great cost to everyone; he feels his own prophecy should come true as well. The friendship between Banquo and Macbeth has been dissolved. Banquo no longer trusts his friend and must be cautious in his presence. Macbeth knows that all the Witches have said has come true and fears Banquo's prophecy will also come true.

Macbeth feels his own sons should succeed him, not Banquo's. Macbeth states his fears and concerns, yet, he does not inform Lady Macbeth of what he has planned. Macbeth feels he must resolve this conflict and he hires murderers to kill Banquo and his son. He feels this will guarantee that his heirs will succeed him. Macbeth does not express remorse or concern over the planning of

Banquo and Fleance's murder, as he did with Duncan's murder. By now, he is so blinded with ambition and power and will stop at nothing to secure his powerful position.

Lady Macbeth and Macbeth discuss the problems they are having even though they have achieved what they wanted. Macbeth feels he has the Banquo situation in hand and assures Lady Macbeth not to worry about it. They both agree that they must continue to hide their true feelings at the banquet. Macbeth says that evil deeds are made stronger through additional evil deeds.

The murderers leave open the possibility of the prophecy being fulfilled because they are unsuccessful with the ambush on Banquo and his son. Banquo is killed, but his son Fleance escapes. Macbeth must still face the fact that Fleance is alive, yet he is delighted that the source has been killed. He does not have to worry about additional sons, only Fleance himself.

This scene also introduces a third murderer. He says he was sent by Macbeth, yet there is no other mention of him in the play. There is much speculation as to the identity of the third murderer. When *Macbeth* is performed on stage, the third murderer is sometimes hooded so that his features cannot be seen.

At the feast, Macbeth's fears and guilt overpower him and he loses control over his inner thoughts. He sees Banquo's ghost. The vision is horrible and he speaks openly to the ghost. Lady Macbeth is unable to control Macbeth, yet she urges him to reign in his fears and remember his guests. Her attempts are futile and she fears he will confess to the murder of Duncan to all the guests. This is the first time Macbeth gives way to a public expression of his inner conflicts; which marks a turning point in the drama. Macbeth continues to manifest his guilt through the vision of the ghost he can only see, and Lady Macbeth asks the guests to leave quickly as Macbeth seems to be getting worse. She has completely lost control of Macbeth.

Almost as quickly as the guests leave, Macbeth's fears surface concerning Macduff's not attending the banquet. Macbeth is fearful that, "Blood, they say: blood will have blood." He is paranoid about everyone and what their behavior means. He must control the situation even if that means killing someone to secure his position and remain in power. Macbeth feels his only recourse is to consult with the Witches as to his fate as they seem to see into the future.

Hecate, the Mistress of the Witches, is agitated that she was not informed as to the events concerning Macbeth. She plans to contribute to his fate by creating a situation that will enable Macbeth to create his own demise. This creates drama and reinforces the power the Witches have in the play.

(The scene with Hecate is not thought to have been in the original text. This has led to speculation that Shakespeare did not write the scene.)

Study Questions

1. As Act III begins Banquo is reflecting on what has happened to Macbeth. What three events does he state and what does he hope for himself?

2. What reason does Macbeth give the Murderers for wanting Banquo killed? What reason does he give for not doing it himself?

3. Why do you think Macbeth does not tell Lady Macbeth about his plan to murder Banquo and Fleance?

4. When Banquo's ghost enters the banquet what is Macbeth's reaction?

5. What does Lady Macbeth say to the guest is the reason for his behavior?

6. Does Macbeth recognize the ghost? How do you know he does?

7. What does Hecate say she is going to do to Macbeth? Why does she think he will respond to her?

8. What does Lennox say about Malcolm, Donalbain, and Fleance?

9. Where has Macduff gone and why?

10. What does Lennox hope for?

Answers

1. Banquo says that Macbeth was made King, Thane of Cawdor and Thane of Glamis. He hopes his sons will be Kings.

2. Macbeth fears for his own life if Banquo lives. Macbeth says that he and Banquo have the same friends and Macbeth would not be able to remain friends with them if he killed Banquo himself.

3. Macbeth either feels that Lady Macbeth may try to talk him out the plot, or he wants to have full control and exclude her from this matter.

4. Macbeth questions who has brought Banquo to the feast and he is very upset.

5. Lady Macbeth tells them that he has suffered from this affliction his entire life and to ignore his behavior.

6. Macbeth recognizes Banquo and says to the ghost that he should not blame him for the murder, "Thou canst not say I did it: never shake Thy gory locks at me."

7. Hecate is going to create a situation that will allow Macbeth to ruin himself. The Witches will make a magic potion that will guide Macbeth's fate by telling him the future. Hecate says mortal men cannot resist knowing the future.

8. Lennox says they have been unjustly accused of murder.

9. Macduff has gone to England to join Malcolm's forces to overthrow Macbeth.

10. Lennox hopes that Scotland will be peaceful again.

Suggested Essay Topics

1. There is a turning point in Act III, Scene 4. What is that turning point and how do you think Macbeth will respond throughout the rest of the drama? Cite examples from the play.

2. Compare and contrast the murders of Banquo and Duncan. How does the murder of Banquo show the change in Macbeth?

Act IV

New Characters:

Apparitions: *visions created by the Witches*

Lady Macduff: *Macduff's distraught wife*

Son: *Macduff's child*

Summary

Scene 1

The Witches are preparing a magic potion and casting a spell. They chant incantations three times to make sure the charm's power will be strong. Macbeth greets the Witches and demands that they give him information about the future. The Witches call upon Apparitions to inform Macbeth of his future.

The first Apparition is that of an armed head saying he should beware of Macduff. The second Apparition is that of a bloody child and it states that no man born of woman will harm Macbeth. The third Apparition is that of a crowned child holding a tree. This Apparition says, "Macbeth shall never vanquished be until Great Birnam Wood to high Dunsinane Hill shall come against him."

Macbeth urges the Witches to give him additional in-

formation about the future. The Witches show him a procession of kings and the last holding a mirror with the reflection of Banquo. The Witches disappear and Macbeth
asks Lennox if he saw the Witches as he entered the room.
Lennox said he did not. Lennox then informs Macbeth
that Macduff has fled to England. Macbeth says he plans
to kill Macduff's family.

Scene 2

Lady Macduff is angered and enraged that her husband, Macduff, has left for England without telling her. She does not know what they are to do now. Ross tries to console her, but she feels her husband is a traitor and a coward. Macduff's son questions his mother about the father's disappearance. She tells him his father is dead; he does not believe her . A messenger arrives and warns Lady Macduff that her life is in danger and she must leave immediately. The Murderers arrive and kill Lady Macduff and her son.

Scene 3

Malcolm and Macduff are in England. Malcolm questions Macduff's motives and wants to make sure that he has not been sent by Macbeth. Malcolm goes on to confess that he has many vices that may make him a far worse King than Macbeth. Macduff's response is that Malcolm is the rightful heir to the throne and Macbeth must be unseated at all cost. Malcolm is convinced that Macduff is sincere and says that the things he said about himself were not true. Malcolm says he is sincere and pure and seeks only good for Scotland.

Ross enters and informs Malcolm and Macduff that Scotland is in a terrible condition. At first Ross hesitates, but then informs Macduff that his family has been brutally murdered. Macduff is shocked and vows to revenge the murder of his family.

Analysis

Hecate knows that Macbeth will not question information given to him but will act upon it. Macbeth is given information that he feels will give him immortality. He is ready to believe only what he feels will benefit him, but he is unable to distinguish the "good" from the "bad". The "Fair is foul and the foul is fair" statement made by the Witches and by Macbeth in this drama has been reinforced in this Act.

Macbeth is no longer capable of making rational judgments or distinguishing good from evil. Obsessed with this knowledge, Macbeth feels he must take quick action to preserve his future. Macbeth feels he must seek Macduff and kill him and his family to insure that the blood line is stopped.

Macbeth is out of control and reacts without thought to his actions. He feels he must spill blood to remain in control and powerful. Once again Macbeth has innocent blood on his hands, and again, he feels no remorse. He is driven by his lust to control the situation and flex his power. The fact that Shakespeare allows the act of the murder to be witnessed as it occurs, rather than have it reported, gives the audience a first-hand impression of the evil nature of Macbeth. The senseless murder of Lady

Macduff and her son contribute to Macbeth's demise and reinforces the flaws in his character.

Malcolm confesses to Macduff that his own character is far worse than Macbeth. He says he has committed crimes worse than Macbeth. Macduff states that he feels Malcolm has the birthright to be the king of Scotland and he knows that he is worthy. Malcolm says that he was only testing Macduff's sincerity. Shakespeare uses this ploy to show that Malcolm is a good man and should be the king. The audience supports Malcolm's efforts to restore Scotland.

The murder of Macduff's family is unnecessary and the act of a tyrant. When Macduff learns that his family has been murdered, he is even more determined to seek revenge on Macbeth. Macbeth is seen as a barbaric killer and Malcolm's cause is reinforced by Macbeth's actions. The murder is the last event that Malcolm and Macduff can allow; they vow to overthrow Macbeth and reclaim Scotland for the people.

Study Questions

1. What are the Witches doing at the beginning of Act IV?

2. What are the three statements made by the Apparitions?

3. What is the significance of the Witches having the Apparitions give the information to Macbeth?

4. What does Macbeth decide to do with the information the Witches have given him?

5. What does Lady Macduff say is the reason for her husband leaving?

6. What does Lady Macduff tell her son about his father? How does he respond to her?

7. What happens to Lady Macduff and her son?

8. Why does Malcolm question Macduff?

9. What is Malcolm's reaction to the news? What is Macduff's?

10. What do Malcolm and Macduff plan to do?

Answers

1. The Witches are standing over a cauldron preparing a spell for Macbeth.

2. The Apparitions say: 1) That Macbeth should beware of Macduff, 2) That no man born of a woman can harm Macbeth, and 3) Macbeth will not be harmed unless Great Birnam Wood comes to high Dunsinane.

3. The Apparitions are dressed in such a way to give insight to Macbeth. He is blinded by his quest for power and does not recognize the significance of the appearance.

4. He plans on going to England to kill Macduff.

5. Lady Macduff feels her husband is scared and is a traitor.

6. Lady Macduff tells her son his father is dead. Her son does not believe her.

7. Lady Macduff and her son are murdered.

8. Malcolm wants to know if Macduff is sincere and that he has not been sent by Macbeth.

9. Malcolm is enraged by the news of Lady Macduff's

death. Macduff is in shock at first then he vows to seek revenge against Macbeth.

10. Malcolm and Macduff plan on killing Macbeth and restoring the peace in Scotland.

Suggested Essay Topics

1. What is the symbolic purpose of each prophecy the Apparitions state in the play? What interpretation can be drawn from the way each are dressed. Do you feel there is a hidden meaning? Cite examples from Act IV.

2. Act IV, Scene 2 is the only scene Lady Macduff is in. Why do you feel Shakespeare chose to have the murder in the scene instead of having it reported, as with Duncan's murder?

Act V

New Characters:

Gentlewoman: *a woman attending Lady Macbeth*

Doctor: *the physician in the castle*

Carthness and Menteith: *nobleman of Scotland in Malcolm's English Army*

Seyton: *an Officer in Macbeth's army*

Siward: *general in the English army fighting with Malcolm*

Young Siward: *Siward's son in the English army with Malcolm*

Summary

Scene 1

The Gentlewoman reports to the Doctor that Lady Macbeth is sleepwalking and her behavior is very strange. The Gentlewoman says that Lady Macbeth gets out of bed, puts on a nightgown, unlocks her closet, writes on a piece of paper, seals the letter and returns to bed.

Lady Macbeth says things that the Gentlewoman refuses to repeat because she fears she will be charged with treason. She urges the Doctor to hear them for himself.

The doctor watches Lady Macbeth and concludes that he cannot treat her illness as she needs the assistance of God. He is very concerned about Lady Macbeth's safety and tells the Gentlewoman to watch her closely.

Scene 2

Menteith, Angus, Lennox and Caithness discuss the battle plans of Malcolm. They plan to meet near Birnam Wood with the others. Macbeth has secured Dunsinane, but his forces are not loyal subjects. Each vow to fight to

the death to regain control of Scotland and overthrow Macbeth.

Scene 3

Macbeth is secure in his castle at Dunsinane. He feels confident because the Witches told him that he cannot be harmed unless the prophecies come to pass. He believes the Witches and has no fear. Macbeth dresses for

battle as the Doctor reveals Lady Macbeth's condition to him. He ask the Doctor to find a cure for his wife. Macbeth leaves for the battle.

Scene 4

Malcolm, Menteith, and Siward are near Birnam Wood. Malcolm tells them they should each cut a branch from a tree from Birnam Wood and use it as camouflage. They prepare to march on to Dunsinane.

Scene 5

Macbeth feels confident that he will overthrow Malcolm in battle. Macbeth hears a cry and discovers that Lady Macbeth is dead. Macbeth responds by saying that life is very short. A messenger arrives to inform Macbeth that the wood of Birnam seems to be moving toward Dunsinane. Macbeth sounds the alarm and prepares to fight.

Scenes 6–8

Malcolm, Siward, and Macduff arrive at Dunsinane and enter Macbeth's castle. Macbeth and Young Siward have a fight and Young Siward is killed. Macduff comes face to face with Macbeth. Macbeth urges Macduff to

leave, as Macbeth feels he has enough of Macduff's blood
on his hands. Macbeth tells Macduff that he cannot be
harmed and cannot be killed by any man born from a
woman. Macduff informs Macbeth that he was not born
of woman, but was "untimely ripped" from his mother's
womb. Macbeth says that what the Witches said had a
double meaning and he did not realize in time the meaning of their prophecy. Macduff calls Macbeth a coward and

coerces Macbeth into fighting him. The two exit and continue their sword fight.

Siward is informed that his son has died valiantly in battle. Macduff returns with the severed head of Macbeth and proclaims Malcolm as the rightful heir to the throne. Malcolm assures the people that Scotland will be restored to a peaceful place when he is King. Malcolm vows to honor the Thanes and kinsmen that helped in the fight against Macbeth with the title of Earl. The drama ends with Malcolm inviting the victors to his coronation at Scone.

Analysis

Lady Macbeth's behavior has been very peculiar, according to the Gentlewoman, and the Doctor is summoned to witness the behavior for himself. Lady Macbeth is responding to her guilty feelings. She is trying to rid herself of her guilt, which takes the form of the blood she is unable to wash from her hands. She confesses to encouraging Macbeth to kill Duncan and refers to Banquo's death as well. She is obsessed with the blood on her hands and she is unable to wash it off. She exclaims, "Out damn spot" as she unsuccessfully tries to remove the blood from her hands. This shows the demise of Lady Macbeth. Her actions and the actions of Macbeth have caused her to loose her mind. The guilt she feels can no longer be controlled; she has lost control of herself.

Macbeth feels confident that he will be safe in battle because of the Witches' prophecy. Macbeth is so self-absorbed with the impending battle that when the Doctor informs him that he cannot help Lady Macbeth, Macbeth simply becomes angry and insists that the Doctor find a cure for her. He then dismisses the doctor and dresses for battle. Macbeth is detached from reality and unaware of the severe condition of his wife. He is so consumed with rage and lust for power that his own wife is no longer important to him. The Witches are the only other source besides himself that Macbeth can trust. He must remain in control at all costs; even if he must spill more blood.

Malcolm and his men ready themselves for battle by using branches from Birnam Wood to shield themselves while approaching Dunsinane. In this way, the Witches' prophecy is fulfilled. Macbeth is informed that Lady Macbeth is dead; he does not even ask how she died. He is only concerned about himself and guarding his power. When the Messenger informs Macbeth that trees seem to be moving toward the castle, Macbeth is angered with him. However, he soon realizes that the Witches' prophecy is coming to pass. His response is to face the battle even if it means his death.

Macbeth has false hopes in his battle with Young Siward because he feels he cannot be harmed by any woman born of man. After Macbeth kills Young Siward, he feels even more confident that he is immortal. He feels he cannot be harmed and will remain in power because of his prophecy.

Macduff faces Macbeth filled with rage and vengeance. When he tells Macbeth that he was "untimely ripped" from his mother's womb, Macbeth realizes that the Witches gave him information that had a double meaning. Macbeth at that moment realizes that his fate has been sealed and he is not immortal.

Macbeth and Macduff fight. They disappear offstage, then return still fighting. Macbeth is then slain and Macduff carries his body offstage. By having the fight momentarily disapear offstage, the drama builds as the audience anticipates the outcome. Since Shakespeare did not have the benefits of modern moviemaking, Macbeth's body had to be taken offstage in order for Macduff to return with the severed head.

The play concludes with Malcom being restored to his rightful place on the throne.

Macbeth is a tragic hero because he has the potential for greatness, but it is undercut by his greed and lust for power. The prophecies of the Witches provide the spark by which Macbeth's soul is set on fire. Once he is presented with the chance to further his own ambition, he lets nothing and no one get in his way. Loyalty becomes treachery and friends become enemies. Even Lady Macbeth's death is naught but a nuisance. Macbeth tells Seyton that she should have waited until tomorrow to die because then he could have spent time mourning for her.

Shakespeare knew how to interpret the complex forces which drive men. On one level, *Macbeth* is about the fight between good and evil. Yet, it is told from the perspective of one man, Macbeth. Even within his own mind, Macbeth is torn between what is right (supporting Duncan) and what is wrong (following his own ambition). Macbeth is not a one dimensional character. He is not wholly evil, there are patches of goodness and regret within him. It is this intricate portrait of Macbeth's personality which adds realism to a play with such supernatural overtones.

Macbeth's road to ruin is twisted and branching. He is offered chances to reverse his course and save himself, but he sticks to the path of personal ambition. Each murderous act leads to another, more horrific than the last. The Witches are often blamed for Macbeth's downfall because he would not have killed the King if he had not heard tales of the future. But, Macbeth does not begin to plan the murder of Duncan until after Malcolm has been named successor. Until that point, Macbeth would have been proclaimed King had Duncan died according to Scottish law. Duncan's announcement usurps that law and Macbeth begins his bloody quest.

In the end, the play has come full circle. At the beginning, Macbeth defends the King against those who would overthrow the crown. In the end Macbeth, who has taken the crown by blood and deceit, is overthrown and rightful rule is restored.

Study Questions

1. What does the Doctor say to Macbeth about Lady Macbeth's condition? What is Macbeth's reaction?

2. What is the Doctor referring to when he says, "Therein the patient Must minister to himself?"

3. What does the Messenger tell Macbeth he sees coming toward Dunsinane? How does Macbeth respond?

4. What does Macduff vow to do to Macbeth and why? Cite an example from Act V.

5. What difference can you cite between Macbeth's army and Malcolm's army?

6. Whom does Macbeth kill in Act V? Do you feel that is important? State your reasons.

7. What does Macbeth say to Macduff about his mortality? What is Macduff's response? How does Macbeth react?

8. What does Ross tell Siward about Siward's son?

9. What does Malcolm say about Macbeth and Lady Macbeth?

10. What title has never been used before in Scotland that Malcolm plans to use on his Thanes and kinsman?

Answers

1. The Doctor says Lady Macbeth is very ill and he cannot cure her himself. Macbeth is angry and does not want to be bothered with this information.

2. The Doctor is saying that Macbeth is trying to tell the doctor how to cure his patient, Lady Macbeth. When in fact Macbeth is the patient himself.

3. The Messenger tells Macbeth that trees are moving toward the castle. Macbeth does not believe him at first; then, sounds the alarm for battle.

4. Macduff vows to have revenge on Macbeth because of the death of his family.

5. Malcolm's army if committed to the cause of saving Scotland. Macbeth's army is fighting for him out of fear they will be killed themselves.

6. Macbeth kills Young Siward. Answers may vary on the response to the second part of the question. The importance of the murder is seen in Macbeth's response after the murder. He states he cannot be killed by a man born of woman. He feels he cannot be harmed.

7. Macbeth tells Macduff that he cannot be harmed by man born of woman. Macduff tells Macbeth that he was ripped from his mother's womb. Macbeth realizes that the Witches have tricked him.

8. Ross tells Siward that his son was killed in battle.

9. Malcolm says that Macbeth is a "butcher" and Lady Macbeth was a "fiend-like queen". He also says that Lady Macbeth took her own life.

10. Malcolm plans to make the Thanes and kinsman Earls.

Suggested Essay Topics

1. Describe Macbeth's reaction to Lady Macbeth's death. Compare his reaction to the reaction he had after the murder of Duncan.

2. Elaborate on the importance of the scene when Lady Macbeth says, "Out damned spot! out, I say! One; two. Why then 'tis time to do't. Hell is murky. Fie, my lord, fie! a soldier, and afeard? What need we fear who knows it, when none can call our pow'r to accompt? Yet who would have thought the old man to have had so much blood in him?" This scene illustrates a change in the character of Lady Macbeth?

Sample Analytical Paper Topics

These analytical papers are designed to review your knowledge of the drama and apply that knowledge to a critical paper. The topics may request that you examine the conflicts, themes, or question a standard theory about the play.

Topic #1

The term tragic hero refers to a central character who has a authoritative status in the drama, but through a flaw in his or her character brings about his or her demise. The flaw may consist of a poor decision that is made and creates a situation the character cannot change or control. The tragic hero recognizes his or her flaw, however there is nothing that can be done to avert tragedy. Macbeth is seen as a tragic hero. Write a paper tracing the sequence of events that contribute to Macbeth's demise and tragic end.

Outline

I.   Thesis Statement: *Macbeth is seen as a tragic hero. He compromises his honor and negates moral responsibility to attain power and position which result in his tragic end.*

II. Definition and characteristics of a tragic hero

   1. Fate

   2. Weakness

   3. Poor decision making resulting in a catastrophe

   4. Realization of flaw but unable to prevent tragedy

III. The Witches

   A. Plan to meet Macbeth

   B. Statement that fair is foul, and foul is fair

IV. Allegiance to Scotland and Duncan

   A. Battle with Macdonwald

   B. Battle with the King of Norway

   C. Duncan's Response

      1. Honor bestowed on Macbeth

      2. Duncan's opinion of Macbeth

V.   Witches on the battlefield

   A. The prophecy

   B. Macbeth's Response

   C. Banquo's Response

VI. Macbeth's meeting with Duncan

    A. Duncan greets Macbeth with respect

    B. Macbeth's reaction to Duncan naming Malcolm as his successor

VII. Decisions made before Macbeth is king

    A. Lady Macbeth's plan

        1. Macbeth's response

        2. Lady Macbeth's Influence on Macbeth

        3. Macbeth's decision

    B. Eve of the Murder

        1. Floating Dagger

        2. Macbeth's reaction

    C. Duncan's Murder

        1. Murder of the guards

        2. Response

    D. Discovery of Duncan's body

        1. Macbeth's reaction

        2. Duncan's sons

        3. Macbeth named as king

VIII. Decisions made as King

    A. Banquo

        1. Fear of prophecy

        2. Hires Murderers

    B. Banquet

        1. Reaction to Murderers

        2. Ghost

    C. Meeting with the Witches

        1. Response to Prophecy

        2. Macduff and family

        3. Leaving for Dunsinane in England

    D. Battle with Malcolm's forces

        1. Dunsinane prophecy

        2. Young Siward

        3. False sense of security

    E. Reactions to Lady Macbeth's illness and death

    F. Meeting Macduff

        1. Guilt

        2. Revealing prophecy to Macduff

        3. Macbeth's Realization that the Witches told him half truths

IX. Macbeth's tragic end

    A. Macduff's victory

    B. Malcolm's speech

Topic #2

Lady Macbeth is seen as a controlling factor in Macbeth's life. She is able to control his actions and events. However, she looses control of Macbeth. Write a paper describing what control she has in Macbeth's life and how the loss of that power contributes to her demise.

Outline

I.   Thesis Statement: *Lady Macbeth's desires for power prompts her interest in controlling Macbeth's actions.*

However, she loses control which contributes to her tragedy.

II. Introduction of Lady Macbeth

  A. Reading Macbeth's letter

  B. Witches prophecy fulfilled

  C. Opinion of Macbeth

  D. Desire for Power

    1. Strength needed

    2. Her plan

III. Meeting with Macbeth

  A. Affection towards each other

  B. Lady Macbeth's plan

IV. Power over Macbeth

  A. Macbeth's Decision about Lady Macbeth's plan

    1. Lady Macbeth's response to Macbeth

      a. Attacks his manhood

      b. Calls him a coward

      c. His fear

      d. Her anger

    2. Macbeth's decision after they speak

      a. Agrees to the plan

      b. Recognizes her strength and vicious nature

  B. Macbeth's vision of the daggers

V. Loss of Control over Macbeth

  A. Duncan's murder

      1. Guards

      2. Voices

      3. Fearful to return to Duncan's chamber

  B. Banquo

      1. Hires Murderers

      2. Murder of Banquo

  C. Banquet

      1. Reaction to Ghost

         a. Lady Macbeth is unable to control Macbeth's response

      2. Confession from Macbeth

      3. Guest leaving upon Lady Macbeth's request

      4. Macbeth turns to the Witches for advice

VI. Decision's made without Lady Macbeth's advice

  A. Banquo's murder

  B. Murder of Macduff's family

  C. Leaving for England

  D. Battle with Malcolm and Macduff

VII. Lady Macbeth's loss of control of her own life

  A. Inability to kill Duncan herself

  B. Taking the bloody daggers back to Duncan's chamber after the murder

  C. Realization she has no control over Macbeth's decisions

  D. Guilt Feelings

VIII. Resolution

    A. Tragic end

       1. Lady Macbeth's

       2. Macbeth's

Topic #3

A motif is a word, image, or action in a drama that happens over and over again. There is a recurring motif of blood and violence in the tragedy Macbeth. This motif contributes to the theme of the drama. In a paper trace the use of blood and violence and cite images that contribute to the theme.

Outline

I. Thesis Statement: *The use of blood and violence occurs throughout the tragedy of* Macbeth. *These images contribute to the understanding of the vicious nature of Macbeth.*

II. The Witches

    A. On the battlefield during the battle

    B. Statement to make foul things fair and fair things foul

    C. Story of the sailor and his wife

    D. Creating a potion

       1. Using blood in the potion

       2. Second Apparition appearing to Macbeth

III. Murders Macbeth commits

    A. Duncan and his guards

       1. Inability to say amen

      2. Voices speaking to Macbeth

      3. Inability to smear blood on guards

      4. Macbeth's description of the murder

  B. Banquo

      1. Murder committed on stage

      2. Vicious nature of the crime

  C. Macduff's family

      1. Murder committed on stage

      2. Defenseless victims D. Young Siward

IV. Lady Macbeth

  A. Plot to murder Duncan

  B. Bloody Daggers

      1. Returning daggers to Duncan's chamber

      2. smearing guards with Duncan's blood

      3. Having the blood on her hands

  C. Guilt feelings

      1. Sleep walking

      2. Confession of the murders

      3. Recalling the events associated with the murders

      4. Inability to wash the guilt, the blood from her hands

      5. Her tragic end

V. Battles Macbeth is involved in

  A. Duncan's Army

      1. Macdonwald's murder

      2. King of Norway

    B. Malcolm's forces

      1. Young Siward's death

      2. Macbeth's forces

    C. Macduff's Revenge

      1. Macbeth's reluctance to battle with Macduff

      2. Macbeth's tragic end

Topic #4

When a comparison is made between two characters the events that happen, the situations that occur, and the characteristics of each character are shown to be similar. When a contrast is made the differences are acknowledge. Write a paper that compares and contrast the characters of Macbeth and Macduff.

Outline

I.   Thesis Statement: *The characters of Macbeth and Macduff are adversaries in the tragedy, however certain similarities can be cited. The differences and similarities contribute to Macbeth's tragic ending and Macduff's resolution.*

II. Similarities between Macduff and Macbeth

    A. Name

    B. Married

    C. Soldiers in Duncan's Forces

    D. Honor

    1. Macbeth's honor at the beginning

    2. Macduff's honor

       a. Loyalty to Scotland

       b. Loyalty to his family

III. Differences in Macduff and Macbeth

  A. Duncan's Murder

    1. Macduff's response

    2. Macbeth's response

  B. Coronation

    1. Macbeth's acceptance of the Crown

    2. Macduff's disagreeing with the selection

       a. Refuses to attend coronation

       b. Leaving for England

       c. Joining Malcolm's fight against Macbeth

  C. Macbeth's Suspicions of Macduff

  D. Witches Warning

    1. Second Apparition

    2. Macbeth orders Macduff's family to be murdered

  E. Death of Wife

    1. Macduff's reaction

       a. Shock

       b. Grief

       c. Wants to know who is responsible

       d. Vow to seek revenge

2. Macbeth's reaction

    a. No emotional response

    b. Does not inquire to the circumstances of her death

IV. Motive for Murder

A. Macbeth murders out of selfish greed and lust for power

B. Macduff murders to avenge the murder of his family

V. Resolution

A. Macduff returns peace to Scotland by killing Macbeth

B. Revenge is achieved

C. Restores Malcolm to the throne of Scotland

Topic #5

The Witches are seen as a force working to bring about the demise of Macbeth. They are known as the antagonist in the drama. They foreshadow events that create suspense in the drama and Macbeth makes decisions based on their prophecies. Write a paper describing how the Witches are a controlling factor in Macbeth's destiny.

Outline

I. Thesis Statement: *Macbeth makes decisions effecting his future based on what the Witches have told him. He guides his destiny based on their prophecies.*

II. Statements made by the Witches in the opening scene

A. "When the hurlyburly's done, When the

battle's lost and won."

B. "Fair is foul, and foul is fair
Hover through the fog and filthy air."

III. Exhibition of Witches' Power

   A. Prophecies

      1. First battle over

      2. Macbeth's title

      3. Macbeth to be made King

      4. Banquo's sons to be Kings

      5. Three Apparitions prophecies

         a. Beware of Macduff

         b. No man born of woman will harm Macbeth

         c. Great Birnam Wood to high Dunsinane Hill

   B. Story of the Sailor

   C. Hecate's speech

   D. Spell cast when potion is made

IV. Macbeth's reaction to prophecies

   A. Disbelief

   B. Anxious for power

      1. Lady Macbeth's plan

      2. Fear of retribution

      3. Decision to kill Duncan

      4. Vision of bloody dagger

   C. Duncan's Murder

      1. Guards murdered

    2. Reaction to the murder

    3. Public reaction to the murder

  D. Banquo

    1. Murder of Banquo

    2. Reaction to Banquo's ghost

    3. Confession at the banquet

  E. Three Apparitions

    1. Decision to leave Scotland for England

    2. Murder of Macduff's family

    3. Engage a battle with Malcolm

  F. Inability to make rash decisions

    1. Murders

    2. Battles

V. Treatment of Lady Macbeth

  A. Affectionate before murder

  B. Avoidance

  C. Disinterested

  D. Lack of grief when he is told of her death

VI. Resolution

  A. Inability to make rational decisions

  B. Guilt feelings consume his mind

  C. Realization of the Witches' prophecies being half-truths

  D. Macbeth's death

SECTION EIGHT

Bibliography

Adventures in English Literature. Shakespeare, William, "Macbeth." Orlando, Florida: Harcourt Brace Jovanovich, 1985.

Boyce, Charles. *Shakespeare A to Z;* New York: Roundtable Press, Inc., 1990.

Goddard, Howard C. *The Meaning of Shakespeare.* Chicago: University of Chicago Press, 1951.

Schmidt, Alexander. *Shakespeare Lexicon and Quotation Dictionary;* Vol. I and II. New York: Dover, 1971.

Taylor, Gary. *Reinventing Shakespeare.* New York: Oxford University Press, 1989.

Introducing...

MAXnotes
EA's Literature Study Guides

MAXnotes™ offer a fresh look at masterpieces of literature, presented in a lively nd interesting fashion. **MAXnotes**™ offer the essentials of what you should know bout the work, including outlines, explanations and discussions of the plot, haracter lists, analyses, and historical context. **MAXnotes**™ are designed to help ou think independently about literary works by raising various issues and thought-rovoking ideas and questions. Written by literary experts who currently teach the ubject, **MAXnotes**™ enhance your understanding and enjoyment of the work.

Available **MAXnotes**™ include the following:

RESEARCH & EDUCATION ASSOCIATION
61 Ethel Road W. • Piscataway, New Jersey 08854
Phone: (908) 819-8880

Please send me more information about MAXnotes™.

Name _____

Address _____

City _____ State _____ Zip _____

Available at your local bookstore or order directly from us by sending in coupon below.

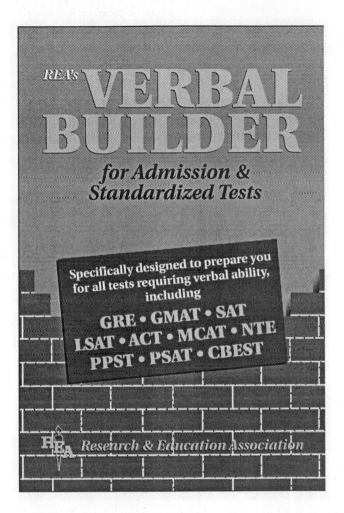

Available at your local bookstore or order directly from us by sending in coupon below.

QUICK
STUDY & REVIEW
FOR THE NEW SAT I®

for students with limited study time and those who want a "refresher" before taking the test

REA *Research & Education Association*

Available at your local bookstore or order directly from us by sending in coupon below.

The High School Tutors

The **HIGH SCHOOL TUTORS** series is based on the same principle as the mor comprehensive **PROBLEM SOLVERS,** but is specifically designed to meet the needs c high school students. REA has recently revised all the books in this series to include expande review sections, new material, and newly-designed covers. This makes the books even mor effective in helping students to cope with these difficult high school subjects.

If you would like more information about any of these books,
complete the coupon below and return it to us or go to your local bookstore.

RESEARCH & EDUCATION ASSOCIATION
61 Ethel Road W. • Piscataway, New Jersey 08854
Phone: (908) 819-8880

Please send me more information about your High School Tutor books.

Name _____

Address _____

City _____ State _____ Zip _____